The Wild Outdoors

GO GEOCACHING!

by
Heather E. Schwartz

CAPSTONE PRESS
a capstone imprint

Published by Capstone Press, an imprint of Capstone
1710 Roe Crest Drive, North Mankato, Minnesota 56003
capstonepub.com

Copyright © 2023 by Capstone. All rights reserved. No part of this publication may be reproduced in whole or in part, or stored in a retrieval system, or transmitted in any form or by any means, electronic, mechanical, photocopying, recording, or otherwise, without written permission of the publisher.

Library of Congress Cataloging-in-Publication Data
Names: Schwartz, Heather E., author.
Title: Go geocaching! / Heather E. Schwartz.
Description: North Mankato, Minnesota : Capstone Press, 2023. | Series: The wild outdoors | Includes bibliographical references. | Audience: Ages 8-11 | Audience: Grades 4-6 | Summary: "Have you always wanted to search for secret treasure? Try geocaching! You can get outside and search for hidden treasure in your very own neighborhood. Learn about geocaching around the world, the supplies you'll need, and the fun that awaits you in this exciting activity!"— Provided by publisher.
Identifiers: LCCN 2021057061 (print) | LCCN 2021057062 (ebook) | ISBN 9781666345711 (hardcover) | ISBN 9781666345728 (paperback) | ISBN 9781666345735 (pdf) | ISBN 9781666345759 (kindle edition)
Subjects: LCSH: Geocaching (Game)—Juvenile literature.
Classification: LCC GV1202.G46 S35 2023 (print) | LCC GV1202.G46 (ebook) | DDC 796.5/8—dc23
LC record available at https://lccn.loc.gov/2021057061
LC ebook record available at https://lccn.loc.gov/2021057062

Image Credits
Associated Press: Greg Wahl-Stephens, 6; Getty Images: AnnaStills, 19, Elva Etienne, 13, EVAfotografie, 14, Imgorthand, 16, pixiecloud, 5, ra-photos, 15, reebinator, Cover, tirc83, 23, Tom Merton, 20, vgajic, 21; Shutterstock: A Club, 7 (bottom), Aigars Reinholds, 29, Alohaflaminggo, 17, Anikakodydkova, 27, Debu55y, 9, Gregory Johnston, 1, karenfoleyphotography, 8, Lucie Parizkova, 11, photocrazed_jls, 22, Postmodern Studio, 18, rbkomar, 25, Tom Wang, 12, Toom Tam, 7 (top)

Editorial Credits
Editor: Erika L. Shores; Designer: Dina Her; Media Researchers: Jo Miller and Pam Mitsakos; Production Specialist: Tori Abraham

All internet sites appearing in back matter were available and accurate when this book was sent to press.

Printed in the United States   5191

Table of Contents

Chapter 1
THE SEARCH IS ON! 4

Chapter 2
THE WORLD'S LARGEST TREASURE HUNT 6

Chapter 3
AN EXCITING ACTIVITY 12

Chapter 4
GETTING OUT THERE 18

Chapter 5
PLAYING BY THE RULES 24

Chapter 6
TIPS AND TRICKS FOR GEOCACHERS 28

    Glossary 30
    Read More 31
    Internet Sites 31
    Index 32
    About the Author 32

Words in **bold** are in the glossary.

Chapter 1

THE SEARCH IS ON!

The words "hidden treasure" might make you think of a pirate's chest filled with shiny gold coins. If you found it, you'd be rich! Finding an actual treasure would be great, but the search itself can be full of excitement.

That excitement is the feeling people who go geocaching chase. They search for hidden containers called geocaches. They use an app or website to check a list of nearby geocaches. Then, they head out to find one. A map, a description of the container the **cache** is in, helpful hints, and nearby landmarks all help in the hunt.

The treasure you find inside a geocache container isn't valuable. It can be anything from stickers to key chains to toy cars. Sometimes, you won't even be able to find the geocache! But you're sure to have lots of fun looking.

Inspecting the contents of a geocache

Chapter 2
THE WORLD'S LARGEST TREASURE HUNT

Geocaching started in the year 2000. A man named Dave Ulmer hid a cache in the woods near Portland, Oregon. Then, he used a **GPS** device to get the coordinates of the location. These numbers told others where on Earth to find his treasure. The rule was they had to use GPS in their search.

Dave Ulmer holding his GPS device

Three days later, a treasure hunter named Mike Teague found a black bucket hidden in the woods. Inside was a videotape, books, **software**, and a slingshot. He'd located the very first geocache. That black bucket kicked off a whole new kind of adventure.

A thick forest of trees and plants can make it extra challenging to find a geocache.

FACT

Geocache is a word that was invented to name this new activity. "Geo" refers to Earth and geography. "Cache" refers to a hiding place or computer storage.

An icebreaker jams an ice shelf on Deception Island, Antarctica.

Today, geocaching is often called the world's largest treasure hunt. People have hidden more than 3 million geocaches all over the world. They are on all seven continents and in 191 different countries.

Some are super hard to find. One of the most difficult is located on Deception Island in Antarctica. The only way to get there is on an icebreaker. It's a special ship that can break through thick ice. Another tough one to reach is in Finland. That one requires diving skills to look around a flooded mine.

But many geocaches are hidden in more pleasant places to visit. If you go to Legoland Discovery Centre in Germany, you can search for one right at the entrance.

Legoland Discovery Centre in Germany

FACT

A fun find in the Netherlands is a geocache designed to look like a real pirate's chest filled with coins and other treasure. It's based on the adventures of Woeste Willem, a character in a Dutch children's book.

You don't have to travel far and wide to go geocaching. Apps and websites make it easy to hunt near your home. You can even choose which kind of **environment** you want to explore. Some geocaches are hidden in the woods. Others are hidden in **urban** areas. There are geocaches practically anywhere you go.

If your search is successful, you'll find loot that's a lot like the treasure hidden in the very first geocache. You might discover a plastic container filled with things like booklets, key chains, ornaments, and small toys. A geocache treasure can be almost anything you can think of! If you take something from the geocache, you must replace it with something else as a trade.

Geocachers can find all sorts of objects inside a container.

Chapter 3
AN EXCITING ACTIVITY

Do you ever get bored running errands with a parent? Maybe you're not big on going to the bank. Maybe you don't like stopping at the grocery store. Go geocaching along the way, and you could turn a dull day into an exciting one.

You can try geocaching when you are out and about in your own city.

You never know where your search for a geocache might take you.

Geocaching gives you new ways to explore your neighborhood. With geocaching on the to-do list, you might drive a different route. You might walk instead of taking a car or bus. During your search, your keen eye might spy some other fun discoveries. Maybe you'll spot a funny bumper sticker. You might see a new store has opened. You could find hidden treasures in your neighborhood before you even reach the geocache.

Do you like hiking in the woods? Running in the park? Playing on the beach? Outdoor activities that send you into nature can be enjoyable on their own. But they're even more fun if you add the excitement of geocaching into the mix.

Imagine trying to find treasure in a pile of rocks. The geocache you're after could be inside a fake stone. Locating a geocache hidden in nature can be especially challenging. Piles of leaves, fallen branches, and old tree stumps can make it hard to spot a geocache.

A geocacher takes notes during her search.

A geocache hidden in a pile of leaves

Tricky Business

Geocachers have reported finding all kinds of human-made fakes while on the hunt. They're meant to throw treasure hunters off the trail and add to the challenge. When geocaching in nature, watch out for false tree branches, 3D printed logs, and hollow bricks made of plastic or foam.

15

Geocaching can be a fun treasure hunt, but it can also be a chance to make the world a better place. More than 363,000 geocachers have volunteered at 18,000 Cache In, Trash Out (CITO) events since 2002. They pick up litter, plant trees, build trails, and help the environment in all sorts of other ways.

When you go geocaching, pay special attention to the environment. Make picking up litter part of your plans. Bring along a bag and gloves, so you can take litter to a proper garbage can. And, of course, don't leave any trash behind.

Some people use a special tool to grab trash off the ground and place it in bags.

Cleaning up trash in nature protects wildlife and plants.

Chapter 4

GETTING OUT THERE

Geocaching starts with technology. You use an app or website, like geocaching.com, to find a geocache to hunt for. If you want to stay near your home, allow your device to access your location. If you want to search in another area, type in the zip code or the name of the town and state. Either way, a list or map of nearby geocaches will pop up on screen. You get to choose the one you want to go after.

A geocaching app on a smartphone

You can go geocaching in a city park or a suburban neighborhood. You might search the wilderness or anywhere you go in the world. That's a lot of choices! Narrow down your options by looking at each geocache's rating for difficulty and **terrain**. The ratings range from 1/1 (easy) to 5/5 (difficult).

Geocachers often use an app on their smartphone when they search for a cache.

A paper map can be helpful during your search.

Before you head out, gather your supplies and gear. No matter where you're going, you'll need a GPS device, like a smartphone. It's a good idea to carry a map and a compass, just in case your phone stops working.

Geocaching near shops and stores? You may not need to pack many supplies if you can easily stop somewhere for snacks and water. Planning to explore the great outdoors? Pack snacks and water in a backpack. Bring a change of clothing and an umbrella in case you get dirty or it rains.

No matter where you're hunting, take along some small toys and trinkets. You may want to trade for things you find in a geocache.

Backpacks with supplies are important to bring along on your search in the outdoors.

A small geocache hangs from a tree.

So what should you look for exactly when you're geocaching? That's hard to say. Geocache containers come in all shapes and sizes. Micro, or nano, geocaches are tiny. Some are about the size of an apple. Other geocaches are so big, you could climb inside.

One thing all geocaches contain is a **logbook**. So you should always bring a pen. Logbooks found in small geocaches often have room only for your name. But in a full-size logbook, you might have space for a whole story about your adventure. The logbook is interesting reading too. It's a written record of everyone who has found the cache. You could read interesting notes from previous geocachers.

Writing in the logbook

FACT

Many people sign "TFTC" next to their names in the logbook. It stands for "Thanks for the cache."

Chapter 5

PLAYING BY THE RULES

One important rule to remember: Take care of the environment. You already know it's important to take your own trash with you. You can go the extra mile by picking up other people's litter too.

But there are more ways to look out for the environment. Suppose you're searching for a geocache in a park. Be careful not to trample plants along the way. What if you suspect a geocache is in a tree? Be sure you don't break any branches in your rush to reach it. You should also cover your tracks if you leave footprints. You don't want to tip-off anyone looking for the same treasure. Otherwise, geocachers who come after you won't get the same kind of challenge.

Walk carefully through areas so as not to disturb plants and animals.

Once you find a geocache, take note of how it was hidden before you move it. After all, you'll need to leave it the same way. Have fun looking over the treasure. But don't take anything you find unless you can leave something too. If you decide to make a trade, be sure the items have equal value. Otherwise, leave something better than what you found.

When you're ready to go, seal up the geocache and hide it again. Now it's the next geocacher's turn to find the treasure!

A geocacher makes a trade.

Hiding a Geocache

Thinking of hiding a geocache yourself? Geocache.com recommends finding 20 geocaches before you take on this challenge. That way, you'll know what it's all about. Always choose a safe spot. And be sure to get permission from the landowner first.

Chapter 6
TIPS AND TRICKS FOR GEOCACHERS

Experienced geocachers have all sorts of tricks for locating treasure. They also find ways to have extra fun on the hunt. Try some of their tips when you head out looking for hidden loot.

- ☑ Be on the lookout for anything that seems out of place. A clamshell in the middle of the forest? That might mark the hiding spot for a geocache.
- ☑ Look high and low, but don't limit your search to the ground. (Also, geocaches are never buried.)
- ☑ Use clues from the app or website you're using.
- ☑ Come up with a special item you can leave behind in each geocache you find. Ideas include business cards, pressed pennies, and tiny homemade sculptures.

Ready to go geocaching? You're sure to find it's a great adventure!

A geocacher reading the logbook

GLOSSARY

cache (KASH)—a hidden place where something is stored

environment (in-VY-ruhn-muhnt)—the natural world of land, water, and air

GPS—stands for Global Positioning System, a radio system that uses signals from satellites to tell you where you are and give you directions to other places

logbook (LOG-book)—a written record

software (SAWFT-wair)—the programs that run on a computer and tell the hardware what to do

terrain (tuh-RAYN)—land of a particular kind

urban (UR-ben)—having to do with cities

READ MORE

Bode, Heather. *Go Hiking!* North Mankato, MN: Capstone Press, 2022.

Harris, Patricia. *What Is Geolocation?* New York: PowerKids Press, 2018.

Mauleón, Daniel. *If You Like Exploring, Adventuring, or Teamwork Games, Try This!* North Mankato, MN: Capstone Press, 2021.

INTERNET SITES

15 Reasons to Love Geocaching
geocaching.com/blog/2017/11/15-reasons-to-love-geocaching/

Discover the Forest: Activities
discovertheforest.org/activities

Geocaching, National Geographic
nationalgeographic.org/encyclopedia/geocaching/

INDEX

apps, 4, 10, 18, 19, 28

compasses, 20

fakes, 14, 15

GPS devices, 6, 20

hiding a geocache, 27

landmarks, 4
litter, 16, 17, 24
logbooks, 23, 29

maps, 4, 18, 20

nature areas, 7, 10, 14, 15, 16, 18, 21, 24, 28

neighborhoods, 13, 18

rocks, 14
rules, 24, 26

sizes, 22, 23
supplies, 20, 21

Teague, Mike, 7
terrain, 18
trading, 10, 21, 26, 27, 28

Ulmer, Dave, 6
urban areas, 10

ABOUT THE AUTHOR

Heather E. Schwartz writes books for kids from her home in upstate New York. She loves writing because she loves learning new things, brainstorming creative ideas, and moving words around on a page. In her spare time, she enjoys baking cookies in fun shapes, throwing holiday parties, walking in the woods, eating cider donuts, and spending time with her family.